AUTH
AND JOY

The Bible in your life

Includes McCheyne Reading Plan

AUTHORITY AND JOY

The Bible in your life

Includes McCheyne Reading Plan

JOHN STOTT & SINCLAIR FERGUSON
Foreword by Don Cormack

In association with

Evangelical Fellowship in
the Anglican Communion

Collection
© Dictum Press, Oxford, UK. First published 2021
dictumpress.com

Foreword
© 2021, Don Cormack

Part 1: *The Authority of the Bible*
First published by Intervarsity Press, USA, 1974
© 1974 InterVarsity Christian Fellowship / USA

Part 2: *Joy in the Bible*
First published in *Table Talk* Magazine, February 2017
© 2017 Sinclair Ferguson / Ligonier Ministries

Part 3: Robert Murray McCheyne Bible Reading Plan
First distributed to the congregation of St Peter's Free Church,
Dundee, 1842
First published in this form as *More Precious than Gold*, IFES
2004

Design by Chris Gander

CONTENTS

Editor's Note

We have followed the NIV in using lower case for 'word' when referring to Scripture; and using upper case when referring to Christ as the Word.

FOREWORD

This powerful little book has a logical progression. We start by embracing the Bible as the authoritative word of God, his own divine self-disclosure in two Testaments: from Creator to Kinsman-Redeemer. This will lead to our being 'surprised by joy', as C S Lewis discovered. There can be no authentic personal transformation or church reformation without an unwavering commitment to God's word. *Sola Scriptura* is the solid rock on which we build.

It is a most timely book. Post-modern relativism has led to rampant individualism. Moral absolutes from our heavenly Father are disappearing in the rear-view mirror. I, ego, have designed my own moral compass. But that compass is seriously faulty, and its magnetic needle needs to be realigned or will take us ever-further off course.

This book lays bare the narcissistic notions and fantasies we harbour about ourselves. We continue to fall for Satan's lie that we can be like God, wise in our own eyes, and accountable to no-one. The result was made clear in Genesis 3. Like Adam and Eve, when we take a look at ourselves, we see only nakedness, shame and alienation. We reach for solace in the cover of 'fig leaves' and the opiates of Vanity Fair.[1]

---

1. Or as John Stott writes: '...to dethrone God and enthrone ourselves not only dispenses with the cross; it also degrades both God and man.' (*The Cross of Christ*, Nottingham, IVP, 2006, p110)

Fulfilment and meaning are not found in a far country of our fantasies, or in the pig-pen of our lusts, but in the loving embrace of our Father-God.

JESUS AND SCRIPTURE

John Stott, with his customary clarity and incisiveness, points out that we should believe in the final authority and divine inspiration of Scripture because Jesus himself did. He constantly appealed to and submitted himself to the word of God. For him, that written word was what we now call the Old Testament. He reminded his disciples, hearers and detractors, time and again, that 'Scripture cannot be broken' (John 10:35), 'must be fulfilled' (Matthew 26:52), 'stands written' (Matthew 4:4ff); and he asks the religious establishment: 'Have you not read the Scriptures?' (Matthew 21:16). His most passionate rebukes were for religious leaders who wilfully set Scripture aside in favour of their own traditions, legalisms and vain-glory.

John Stott explains how Jesus clearly anticipated the New Testament being written. Jesus specifically chose, commissioned and authorized Apostles to be his representatives and spokesmen (just as God had done with the Old Testament prophets), assuring them that they would be uniquely equipped and enabled by the Holy Spirit to remember everything he, Christ, had taught them, and all they had personally witnessed, in particular his resurrection (John 1:14; 15:15; 21:24-25; Revelation 1:1-3; 22:18-19). In short, to receive the Apostolic gospel would be to receive Jesus' own teaching and testimony (John 16:12-15, Acts 2:42). Each Testament is an account of God's sovereign, redemptive purpose centred in Christ, seamlessly authored by the Holy Spirit, mutually foretelling and fulfilling, referring and affirming.

The centrality of biblical authority is not some dry, academic debate, but vital truth for the integrity of the church, as well as for our personal Christian lives. As Sinclair Ferguson's article affirms, biblical authority and Christian joy go hand in hand. The Scriptures

BIBLICAL AUTHORITY AND CHRISTIAN JOY GO HAND IN HAND

call us to 'rejoice in the Lord always', to enjoy and glorify him with our whole being for who he is, all he has revealed, and all he has done. This confidence in Scripture's authority is the only ground for our enduring faith in the truth of the gospel of God's grace; for our assurance, comfort and joy in God's redeeming love (John 1:14).

Enjoying daily companionship with our Father God is an act of the will. Our troubled, wayward hearts and minds need to be daily educated and renewed by the word of God. As someone has said, 'God comes to us clothed in the Holy Scriptures'. The Scriptures speak to our hearts of the unfathomable depths of God's self-giving love at Calvary. The Cross is where the supreme revelation of God's character is seen in all its glory, in the sheer extremity of his divine love and holiness. The best space in which to allow God to speak with us, and for us to examine our hearts, is in unhurried silence. Then we can sing with gratitude and joy:

> *My name from the palms of his hands*
> *Eternity will not erase;*
> *Impressed on his heart it remains,*
> *In marks of indelible grace...*[2]

Our God and the angelic hosts of heaven join with us, rejoicing in our salvation and preparation for 'the eternal weight of glory'. Some of us were lost like sheep, absorbed in 'licking the earth'[3] satisfying our appetites, mindlessly wandering away from the Good Shepherd. Others, through no fault of their own, were carelessly dropped, left to roll away into dark and dirty places. And all of us have been plain rebellious; wilfully and foolishly insisting on doing it 'my way'. Now we joyfully join with former slave-trader John Newton, and sing 'Amazing grace, how sweet the sound that saved a wretch like me', yet each of us must add 'prone to wander, Lord, I feel it, prone to leave the God I love.'[4] We know ourselves to have been sheep in need of a shepherd, cosmic orphans in need of an eternal Father, sinners in need of a Saviour.

FINDING JOY

There are joyful surprises to be discovered in God's word. I found this over and over again during my time

---

2. Augustus Toplady (1740-1778)
3. Blaise Pascal: (1623-1662) Pensées #666
4. Robert Robinson (1735-1790)

in Cambodia. I met Dee when I was seeking to bring God's word to the humble trishaw-drivers plying the streets of Phnom Penh. Dee was curious about our church and those who had become Christians. He knew what the requirements were for Buddhists and Muslims, and asked about the do's and don't's for Christians. I told him how Jesus, the visible image of the one eternal God, had answered his very question: 'Love the Lord your God with all your heart and with all your soul and with all your mind and with all your strength; and love your neighbour as yourself' (Mark 12:28-31). After some moments of silence, Dee declared, 'No man could have come up with such an idea. Love God with my whole being, and what I wish for myself I must do for

THESE WORDS WERE TRUE, AUTHORITATIVE, AND JOYFULLY COMPELLING

others? Those words could have come only from God!' The Holy Spirit had confirmed to Dee that these words spoken by both prophet and apostle were from God himself: true, authoritative, and joyfully compelling. It was everything he wanted to know; it resonated in his heart; it perfectly expressed his own desire for God. It was how he wanted to live and worship. This lowly trishaw-driver had seen the pathway to joy in God's own self-disclosure to him, through these verses of Scripture. It was not by accumulating merit, but by receiving and sharing the love of God in Christ crucified.

Sinclair Ferguson reminds us that joy is also to be found through tribulation and suffering. To grasp this, we need to look beyond the horizon, beyond the sun; to fix our eyes on Jesus who suffered the agony of total desolation in the darkness and God-forsaken silence of Gethsemane. He became our sin-bearer, our Kinsman-Redeemer, our scapegoat: tied up, and led away to die for the sins of the people.

From eternity past, God the Father had been pouring out his love on God the Son in the fellowship of God the Holy Spirit. But on the cross, the Father's face is turned away. The incarnate Son suffers and dies in substitutionary atonement for the sin of fallen mankind; our death, our curse – once and for all, propitiating, absorbing, the righteous anger of a holy God.

We hear our Saviour's aweful words, crying out to the Father, 'My God, my God, why have you forsaken me?' He died so that we in death, at the final judgement, need never cry those terrible words. He bore death on the cross 'for the joy set before him… scorning its shame, and sat down at the right hand of the throne of God. Consider him who endured such opposition from sinful men that you will not grow weary and lose heart…' (Hebrews 12:2-3). There is joy in tribulation because our perspective is not limited to beneath the sun, but fixed on him who is seated at the right hand of God with wounds in his hands, his side and his feet, blessed wounds which he will carry for all eternity.

Only two of Cambodia's pastors survived the Khmer Rouge's Killing Fields.[5] One was Pastor

---

5. Cambodia was under the rule of the Khmer Rouge reign of terror from 1975-1979, during which over two million people died. See note 6.

Hom ('hom' sounds like the Cambodian word for 'fragrant').[6] Along with the bedraggled remnants of his little flock, he had crawled through mine-infested jungle, past killer-patrols and desperate brigands, finally making it to a crowded refugee-camp just over the Thai border. Miraculously, I was led to them one hot, dusty afternoon. They were sitting together in the shade of some bamboo, all skin and bone, the black rags of their Khmer Rouge clothing hanging on their shoulders. All had experienced unspeakable pain and horror. But on receiving replacements for Cambodian Bibles and hymn books, long-since confiscated or lost, they were at once down on their knees singing:

> *The love of God, how rich and pure*
> *how measureless and strong.*
> *It shall for evermore endure,*
> *the saints' and angels' song.*[7]

Their first thought was to worship, to extol the love of God. And I recalled words from the Book of Daniel: 'They came forth from the flames with no smell of the burning upon them' (Daniel 3:27b). They bore instead the fragrance of the knowledge of God who had

---

6. Don Cormack met Pastor Hom in 1979, while Don was working in the refugee camps all along the Thai/Cambodia border. See *Compelling Stories from Pol Pot's Cambodia* (Dictum, 2022).
7. This hymn, composed by American pastor, Frederick M Lehman in 1917 was inspired by the words of a Jewish acrostic poem *Haddamut*, written in Aramaic in 1050 by Rabbi Meir ben Isaac Nehorai. From ancient Hebrew to modern Cambodian in a grim 20th Century refugee camp, worshipping the same God. Ours truly is a sung faith!

walked with them through that fiery crucible. Soon, I could no longer see them as a great crowd of refugees had gathered around them, wondering what on earth these people had to sing about. Unsurprisingly, a church soon grew up around these 'ransomed of the Lord'; among those who, as Ferguson reminds us from Isaiah 51:11, are '...crowned with everlasting joy' and for whom 'sorrow and mourning will disappear [for] they will be filled with joy and gladness.'

'TODAY' IN SCRIPTURE

Then we conclude with Robert Murray McCheyne's Bible Reading Plan with its four simultaneous 'great beginnings', as John Stott explains. Bible reading can at times become burdensome and hard-going, the Bible's very cover a seemingly unbearable weight to lift open. I love the way McCheyne sympathises with that (p55). 'My desire', he wrote to his congregation, 'is not to cast a snare on you, but to be a helper of your joy.'

Multitudes have been blessed by the discipline of this reading plan since McCheyne first wrote it for his congregation at St Peter's Free Church, Dundee, Scotland in 1842. Through this vital means of grace, the Lord will meet with us, speak to us, and daily

A GODLY LIFE IS BUILT ONE DAY AT A TIME

wash from our feet the filth we pick up as we make our way through this world.

The biblical concept upon which McCheyne's plan is based is the importance of 'today', for a godly life is built one day at a time.

Again and again in Scripture, the word 'today' appears or is implied: 'Today, if you hear his voice...', 'Give us this day...', 'Sufficient unto the day...', 'Encourage one another daily...', 'Do not let the sun go down on your anger...' With God's enabling grace, I can trust him for this day, focus on this one tiny microcosm of my life; then tomorrow, when it comes, we do it all over again.

God's promises, along with his warnings and admonitions are sealed with the blood of his Son. Let us constantly nourish ourselves in his word, and experience the peace and joy of our salvation; that divine fellowship which springs from a winsome, teachable, childlike spirit, and a humble and submissive heart. May it become the fount of your everlasting joy as you fulfil your eternal calling to be a child of God. And may this short book be a blessing to you in that endeavour.

Don Cormack
Lent 2021

Don Cormack, a retired Anglican minister, served with OMF International. He was forced to flee Cambodia in 1975, just prior to the Khmer Rouge entering Phnom Penh, returning in 1992, following the Paris Peace Accords. His chronicle of the Cambodian Church, Killing Fields, Living Fields *was first published in 1997.*

PART 1

THE AUTHORITY OF
THE BIBLE

THE AUTHORITY OF THE BIBLE

John Stott's address, first delivered to students at the Urbana Missions Convention, 1974, is timeless in its appeal and its importance.

A uthority is a dirty word today – disliked, even detested. I doubt if any other word arouses more instant aversion among the young and the radical of all kinds. Authority smacks of establishment, of privilege, of oppression, of tyranny. And whether we like it or not, we are witnessing in our day a global revolt against all authority, whether of the family, the college, the bosses, the church, the state, or God.

OUR DOUBLE STANCE

Now the Christian is always in an ambivalent position vis-à-vis the mood of the world. We have to avoid the two extremes of an uncritical acquiescence and of an equally-uncritical rejection. On the one hand, we should respond to the contemporary world with sensitivity,

> *WE HAVE TO AVOID TWO EXTREMES OF ACQUIESCENCE AND REJECTION*

listening, striving to understand, and, where possible, agreeing. On the other hand, we must continue to stand over against the world, evaluating secular society by our own objective Christian criteria, and, where necessary, disagreeing, protesting and rejecting. It is not the calling of the church to sing along with whatever is happening. For that is, to use a biblical metaphor – to be a reed shaken with the wind.

If we adopt this double stance toward the world, what will happen to the debate about authority? It would be foolish to give the whole anti-authority movement a blanket condemnation. Indeed, some of it is responsible, mature and truly Christian. It arises from the Christian understanding of human nature, and our dignity as creatures made in God's likeness. It protests against the dehumanization of human beings and sets itself against all injustice and discrimination which insult both God the Creator and man the creature. It seeks to protect human beings against exploitation by 'the system,' 'the machine,' 'the institution'. It longs to see people liberated to enjoy their God-given freedom.

It is right to detect a grievous misuse of authority when civil rights and freedom of speech are denied

IT IS RIGHT TO DETECT A GRIEVOUS MISUSE OF AUTHORITY

to citizens; when a racial or tribal or religious minority is victimized; when an economic system holds people in bondage to materialism; or when education is hardly distinguishable from indoctrination. In such situations, when non-Christians protest, Christians should not be ashamed to be associated with the protest. Indeed, we should have initiated it ourselves.

4

But much of today's anti-authority mood is more radical still. Sometimes it is a plea, not for the true human liberty which God intends, but for anarchy (a total abolition of the rule of law) and for an individual human autonomy (everyone a law to himself) which God never intended. Christians cannot go along with secularists when they agitate for unlimited permissiveness in social and ethical terms, nor when they foolishly imagine that 'free thought' is intellectual freedom, or that 'free sex' is moral freedom.

MEANING, AND THE AUTHORITY OF SCRIPTURE

The meaning of Scripture is further challenged by those who want to undermine 'authorial intent'; that is, those who believe that the reader's interpretation of a text (any text: whether the Bible, or a novel) is just as valid as the author's intended meaning. This takes us back to our childhood nursery rhyme about Humpty Dumpty, who in Alice's dream said that words could be given whatever meaning anyone liked. Humpy Dumpty sounded ludicrous back in 1860s Oxford, where the book was written. But author Charles Doddridge, a maths lecturer at Oxford University (known better by his pen name Lewis Carroll) could see the world of today, which gives validation to this.

For Christians, the meaning of words has great importance. God has given us Scripture as his written word.

THE MEANING OF WORDS HAS GREAT IMPORTANCE

And neither truth nor righteousness is relative, since God has given us (by revelation) absolute standards both of what is true and of what is right. This brings us straight to our subject: *Jesus Christ and the authority of the Word of God*.

The eighteenth century essayist, Charles Lamb, said that 'if Shakespeare were to come into this room, we should all rise up to meet him, but if that Person [Jesus Christ] were to come into it, we should all fall down and try to kiss the hem of his garment.' For myself I think we would do more than kiss his clothing. We would surely go on to acknowledge him as our Lord. We would kneel beside Thomas saying 'My Lord and my God' and beside Saul of Tarsus saying 'Lord, what do you want me to do?'

This is the only possible attitude of mind in which to approach our study of Jesus Christ and the authority of the Word of God, for belief in the authority of Scripture and submission to the authority of Scripture follow on from our submission to the lordship of Jesus.

Let me enlarge on this theme and then see what we can learn from it.

ENLARGING ON OUR THEME

Why do evangelical Christians believe that the Bible is God's Word written, inspired by his Spirit and authoritative over our lives? We do not take a blindfold leap into the darkness and resolve to believe what we suspect is incredible.

Nor do we believe it because the universal church taught this for eighteen centuries (though long tradition should not lightly be set aside). Nor is it because God's word authenticates itself to us as we read it today – by the majesty of its themes, by the unity of its message and by the power of its influence (though it does all this, and more). No. The overriding reason for accepting the divine inspiration and authority of Scripture is plain loyalty to Jesus.

We believe *in* Jesus, and we believe Jesus. We are convinced that he came from heaven and spoke from God. He said so: 'No one knows the Father except the Son' (Matthew 11:27). Again, 'my teaching is not mine, but his who sent me' (John 7:16) and 'we speak of what we know, and bear witness to what we have seen' (John 3:11). So we are prepared to believe what he taught for the simple reason that it is he who taught it. That is why we want to bring our minds into submission to his mind, and to conform our thoughts to his thoughts. It is from Jesus that we derive our understanding of God and ourselves, of good and evil, of duty and destiny, of time and eternity, of heaven and hell. Our understanding of *everything* is conditioned by what Jesus taught. And this *everything* means *everything*: It includes his teaching about the Bible. We have no liberty to exclude anything from Jesus's teaching and say, 'I believe what he taught about this, but

WE HAVE NO LIBERTY TO EXCLUDE ANYTHING FROM JESUS'S TEACHING

not what he taught about that.' What right have we to be selective? We have no competence to set ourselves up as judges and decide to accept some parts of his teaching while rejecting others. All Jesus' teaching was true. It is the teaching of none other than the Son of God.

What, then, *did* Jesus teach about the Bible? We have to remember that the Bible consists of two halves, the Old Testament and the New Testament. And the way he endorsed each is different – inevitably so because the New Testament had not yet been written.

THE OLD TESTAMENT

Jesus made several direct statements about the Old Testament's divine origin and permanent validity. He had not come to abolish the law and the prophets but to fulfil them. Indeed, 'till heaven and earth pass away, not an iota, not a dot, will pass from the law until all is accomplished' (Matthew 5:17-18; cf. Luke 16:17). Again, 'Scripture cannot be broken' John 10:35).

To these direct statements we should add the indirect evidence provided by the formulas he used to introduce his Scripture quotations. For example, he prefaced a quotation from Psalm 110 by the expression 'David himself, speaking by the Holy Spirit, declared' (Mark 12:36), and he attributed a statement about marriage written by the author of Genesis to the Creator himself, who in the beginning made human beings male and female (Matthew 19:4-5).

More impressive than what Jesus *said* about Scripture, however, is the way he personally *used* it. His high view of Scripture as God's written Word is shown in the important place it occupied in his own life and ministry. He did not just talk about Scripture; he believed it and acted on it himself. Let me give you three examples. In each there was a potential

> *JESUS'S HIGH VIEW OF SCRIPTURE IS SHOWN IN HIS OWN LIFE AND MINISTRY*

element of uncertainty, a question or problem. In each he answered the question and resolved the problem by an appeal to Scripture. In each, therefore, his personal submission to Scripture is plainly seen:

1. **The area of personal duty**. What did the Lord God require of Jesus? What were to be the standards and values by which he would live his life? The devil raised such questions as these with him in the wilderness of Judea, as he had raised them with Adam and Eve in the Garden of Eden several millennia previously. The devil tempted Jesus to disobey God, to doubt God and to desert God. But whereas in the garden Eve succumbed to the insinuations of Satan, in the wilderness Jesus resisted them. 'Be gone, Satan' he cried. Why? 'Because it stands written [in Scripture] 'you shall not.' The plain prohibitions of Scripture were enough for Jesus. For him what Scripture said, God said. There was no place for argument and no room for negotiation. He was determined to

obey God his Father, and he knew that in order to do so, he must submit to Scripture and do what stands written there.

2. ***The area of official ministry***. The four gospels do not describe the process by which Jesus came to an understanding of who he was (his identity) and what he had come to do (his role). It seems very probable, however, that it was through meditation on the Old Testament Scriptures. Certainly before his public ministry began, he knew he was the Son of God, the anointed King, the suffering servant and the glorious Son of Man described by different psalms and prophets. Also, he had so fused these different pictures in his mind that he knew he could enter his glory only if he were first to serve, suffer and die. This self-understanding was confirmed to him at his baptism when the Father's voice acclaimed him saying: 'You are my beloved Son in whom I am well pleased.'

But immediately afterward, the devil threw him into a painful identity crisis, challenging him repeatedly in the wilderness – 'If you are the Son of God – if...if...if...' – attempting to sow in his mind seeds of doubt about his identity and role.

And these temptations continued throughout his ministry. Another crisis came at Caesarea Philippi when Jesus first taught the apostles openly, 'the Son of Man must suffer many things and be rejected and be killed,' and Peter rebuked him, 'God forbid, Lord! This shall never happen to you' (Matthew 16:22). Immediately Jesus rounded on Peter with the fierce words, 'Get behind me, Satan!' He recognized in the words of Peter the voice of the devil. It was the same question of his identity and role.

Peter did it again in the Garden of Gethsemane when he drew his sword and tried to avert the arrest of Jesus. Jesus said to him, 'Put your sword back into its place ... Do you think that I cannot appeal to my Father, and he will at once send me more than twelve legions of angels? But how then should the Scriptures be fulfilled, that it must be so?' (Matthew 26:52-54).

This 'must' ('the Son of Man *must* suffer,' and 'it must be so') has only one explanation. It was a necessity laid upon him by Scripture. Scripture revealed to him his messianic role. And he was determined voluntarily to fulfil it, because, as far as he was concerned, what Scripture said, God said.

3.   **The area of public controversy**. Every reader of the Gospels quickly notices how many public debates they include. Regarding Jesus as a particularly wise rabbi, individuals would come to him with their questions. Sometimes they were genuine inquiries like, 'what must I do to inherit eternal life?' On this occasion Jesus' reply is significant to our theme. He responded with a counter question: What is written in the law?' (Luke 10:25-26).

Trick questions

Jesus was also drawn into disagreement with the religious authorities, in particular the rival groups known as the Pharisees and the Sadducees. Both groups criticized him and came to him with their trick questions.

The Pharisees complained that his followers did not observe the traditions of the elders in ceremonial matters like washing their hands and their vessels. In his reply Jesus accused them of rejecting the commandment of God and making void the word of God in order to keep their traditions (Mark 7:1-13). The Sadducees, on the other hand, who did not believe in survival or resurrection, emphasized the problems an afterlife would create. They asked Jesus what would happen to a poor woman who had seven husbands, one after the other, each of whom she outlived. Whose wife would she be in the resurrection? Would she have one of them (which would mean the other six were out of luck) or none of them (which would be a bit hard all around) or all seven (which somehow does not sound decent)? They thought they could dispose of the doctrine of the resurrection by ridicule. But Jesus said to them, 'Is not this why you are wrong, that you know neither the Scriptures nor the power of God?' (Mark 12:18-27).

BOTH GROUPS SHOWED A CAVALIER TREATMENT OF THE WORD OF GOD

Both religious groups showed a cavalier treatment of the word of God. The Pharisees *added* to Scripture (namely, their traditions) while the Sadducees *subtracted* from Scripture (namely, the supernatural). Neither of them gave Scripture respect as God's word written. Jesus accused the Pharisees of making it void and the Sadducees of being ignorant of it. In both cases he made Scripture the judge of their teaching.

In each of these three examples above — concerning the realms of personal duty, official ministry and public controversy — there was a question, a problem, a dispute. And in each case Jesus turned to Scripture to answer the question, to solve the problem, to settle the dispute. When the devil tempted him, he resisted the

> ## HE RESISTED THE TEMPTATION WITH 'IT STANDS WRITTEN'

temptation with 'It stands written.' When the apostles rejected the necessity of his sufferings, he insisted that the Scriptures must be fulfilled. When the Jewish leaders criticized his teaching, he criticized their treatment of Scripture.

Jesus endorsed the Old Testament as the word of God. Both in his view of Scripture and in his use of Scripture, he was entirely and reverently submissive to its authority as to the authority of God's own word. The disciple is not above his teacher, nor is the servant above his lord. How then can we, the disciples of Jesus, possibly have a lower view of Scripture than our Teacher himself had? How can we, the servants of Jesus, allow Scripture to occupy a smaller place in our lives than it occupied in the life of our Lord himself?

Two escape routes?

There are only two possible escape routes from this obligation. Let's look at them.

1. To say that Jesus did not know what he was talking about, that the Incarnation imprisoned him in the limited mentality of a first-century Palestinian Jew, and that consequently he believed the Old Testament as they did, but that he, like them, was mistaken.

2. To say that Jesus *did* know what he was talking about, that he actually knew Scripture to be unreliable, but that he still affirmed its reliability because his contemporaries did, and he did not want to upset them.

According to the *first*, Jesus could not help his erroneous teaching; according to the *second* it was deliberate. These theories portray Jesus as either deceived or a deceiver. They are incompatible with his claims to speak what he knew (John 3:11) — that is, to bear witness to the truth, and to be the truth (John 18:37; 14:6) — and with his known hatred of all hypocrisy and deceit. They are unacceptable to anybody who has been led by the Holy Spirit to say 'Jesus is Lord' (1 Corinthians 12:3). We must continue to affirm that Jesus knew what he was teaching, that he meant it, and that what he taught and meant is true.

THE NEW TESTAMENT

The argument here is different, but equally compelling. If Jesus endorsed the Old Testament, setting his stamp of approval on it, he also foresaw the writing of the Scriptures of the New Testament, parallel to the Scriptures of the Old Testament. Indeed, he not only foresaw it, he actually intended it, and he deliberately made provision for it by appointing and authorizing his apostles.

Apostle is the title which Jesus himself chose for the Twelve, in order to indicate their role. 'He called his disciples,' Luke writes, 'and chose from them twelve, whom he named apostles' (Luke 6:13). Mark adds that he appointed them to be sent out to preach' (Mark 3:14). The verb *apostello* means 'to send,' and the mission on which he proposed to send them was essentially a teaching and preaching mission.

It is true that the word *apostolos* seems to have been used once in the New Testament to describe every Christian (John 13:16), for Jesus sends us all 'into the world' as his ambassadors, and we are all called to have some share in the apostolic mission of the church (John 17:18; 20:21). It is

> WE ALL SHARE IN THE APOSTOLIC MISSION OF THE CHURCH

also true that the same word *apostolos* is used once or twice in the expression 'apostles of the churches' (2 Corinthians 8:23; cf. Philippians 2:25), which seems to refer to what we would call 'missionaries'— that is, Christians sent on a particular mission by the church (see Acts 13:3; 14:15). Nevertheless, the New Testament almost universally restricts the word *apostolos* to the special apostles of Christ, namely, the original Twelve, together with a very small number of later additions, notably Paul (see Galatians 1:1) and James, the Lord's brother (Galatians 1:19).

There was a double background to the word *apostle* — ancient and contemporary — which helps us understand why Jesus chose it.

First, the ancient background. The ancient background is biblical, namely, the repeated Old Testament use of the verb to send in reference to the prophets of God. 'Come,' said God to Moses, 'I will send you to Pharaoh' (Exodus 3:10); and later Moses insisted over against his jealous rivals, 'You shall know that the LORD has sent me ... and that it has not been of my own accord' (Numbers 16:28-29). It was even clearer in the case of the great prophets of the seventh and eighth centuries BC. 'Whom shall I send?' God had asked in Isaiah's hearing. 'Send me,' Isaiah had replied (Isaiah 6:8). 'To all to whom I send you, you shall go,' he said to Jeremiah (Jeremiah 1:7), and to Ezekiel: 'Son of man, I send you to the people of Israel' (Ezekiel 2:3).

Several times the word of God came to Jeremiah saying, 'I have sent to you all my servants the prophets, sending them persistently' (Jeremiah 35:15). In each case the sending is not a vague dispatch but a specific commission to assume the role of a prophet and to speak God's word to the people. It is evident that when Jesus gave to the Twelve the title 'apostles' and sent them out to teach, he was likening his apostles to God's prophets and indicating that they were to speak in his name and carry his word to others. The prophets of the Old Testament and apostles of the New Testament were equally organs of divine

JESUS'S APOSTLES ARE THE FOUNDATION ON WHICH THE CHURCH IS BUILT

revelation. As such they are the foundation on which the church is being built (Ephesians 2:20; 3:5).

Second, the contemporary background. The word *apostolos* is the Greek equivalent of the Aramaic *shaliach*, and *shaliach* already had a well-defined meaning as a teacher sent out by the Sanhedrin to instruct the Jews of the Dispersion. As such the *shaliach* carried the authority of those he represented, so that it was said, 'the one who is sent is as he who sent him.' In the same way Jesus sent out his apostles to represent him, to bear his authority and teach in his name, so that he could say of them: 'He who receives you receives me' (Matthew 10:40; also see John 13:20).

Both the prophetic and the rabbinic background throw light on the meaning of the word apostolos. The apostle was a specially-chosen emissary, the bearer of another and higher authority, the herald of a given message. When we turn to the New Testament itself and to the New Testament understanding of the apostles of Jesus, we see that they were given a threefold equipment for their task, which together render them a unique and irreplaceable group. These three qualifications were (i) their personal commission, (ii) their historical experience, and (iii) their special inspiration.

First, their personal commission. No apostle was self-appointed, or appointed by someone else, or even by the church. They were all personally chosen, commissioned and authorized by Jesus. This was clear in the case of the Twelve. Out of a much wider constituency of disciples Jesus 'chose from them twelve, whom he named apostles' (Luke 6:13). It was equally clear in the case of Paul, although Christ chose him after the ascension. One of the accounts of his conversion which Luke preserves in Acts includes the very words of apostolic commissioning, *ego apostello se*, 'I apostle you' or 'make you an apostle' (Acts 26:17). And in his letters Paul not only asserts his apostleship ('Paul an apostle of Christ Jesus by the will of God') but vigorously defends it (for example, in Galatians 1:1, 'Paul, an apostle – sent not from men nor by man, but by Jesus Christ and God the Father, who raised him from the dead').

Second, their historical experience. This, too, is very clear in the case of the Twelve. Jesus appointed them, writes Mark, 'to be with him, and to be sent out to preach' (Mark 3:14). These two purposes belonged together. They could be sent out to preach only after they had been with him,

for their preaching was to be a witness to him,
out of their own experience, from what they had
seen and heard. 'You also are witnesses,' Jesus
was to say to them later, because you have been
with me from the beginning' (John 15:27).

So when the time came for somebody to replace
Judas, the essential qualification Peter laid down
was that he must 'have accompanied us during
all the time that the Lord Jesus went in and out
among us, beginning from the baptism of John
until the day when he was taken up from us,'
and in particular that he must become with us
a witness to his resurrection' (Acts 1:21-22). Saul
of Tarsus seems to have been the last apostle to
be appointed. Although he was not one of the
Twelve and did not know Jesus during his public
ministry, yet he had been granted a resurrection
appearance. Without this he could not have been
an apostle. 'Am I not an apostle? he cried. 'Have I
not seen Jesus our Lord?' And again, 'Last of all, as
to one untimely born, he appeared also to me. For I
am the least of the apostles' (1 Corinthians 9:1; 15:8,
9). The same was true of James (1 Corinthians 15:7).

Third, their special inspiration of the Holy Spirit.
Of course all Christians have received the Holy
Spirit to dwell within us, to show Christ to us
and make us like Christ, but Jesus promised the
apostles an unusual ministry of the Holy Spirit,
relating to their teaching ministry. The Spirit

would bring to their remembrance all that Jesus had said to them, and he would teach them 'many things which Jesus had not said to them because they had been unable to bear them. In fact, he would guide them into all the truth (John 14:25, 26; l6:12-13). These great promises evidently looked forward to the writing of the Gospels (in which Jesus' teaching was remembered) and of the Epistles (in which Jesus' teaching was supplemented).

In these three ways Jesus made a purposeful preparation for the writing of the New Testament Scriptures. He gave his apostles a personal commission, an historical experience, and a special inspiration. Each was a gift from Jesus to them, and each was designed to equip them for their unique role as his apostles.

The next point to notice is that the apostles understood these things. They were conscious of the unique position to which Jesus had appointed them. They exercised the authority which he had given them, and they expected the churches to acknowledge it also. We see this in their letters, which they ordered to be read publicly in the early Christian assemblies, alongside the Old Testament Scriptures (for example, Colossians 4:10; 1 Thessalonians 5:27; Revelation 1:3).

Paul stated that his message was 'the word of God' (1 Thessalonians 2:13) and that the very words in which it was communicated were 'not taught by human wisdom but taught by the Spirit' (1 Corinthians 2:13). This is a claim not to divine revelation only, but to verbal inspiration.

Further, Paul issued commands and required obedience, for he could say, 'What I am writing to you is a command of the Lord' (2 Thessalonians 3:6-15; 1 Corinthians 14:37). When he went to Galatia, they received him 'as an angel of God, as Christ Jesus' (Galatians 4:14), that is, as if he were himself God's messenger, God's Christ. He did not rebuke them for this. Far from it. His complaint was not that they formerly regarded him thus, but that now the false teachers had made them less ready to defer to his authority. And he evidently told the Corinthians that Christ was speaking in and through him, for he referred to their desire for proof that this was so (2 Corinthians 13:3; see also v10).

Turning to other apostles, Peter identified the good news which he had preached and by which his converts had been born again as 'the living and abiding word of God' (1 Peter 1:22-25). And John declared not only that what he and his fellow apostles proclaimed was what they had seen and heard, (John 1:1-4), but that this original teaching of the apostles was normative for all times. Consequently, he kept calling his readers back to 'what they heard from the beginning' (1 John 2:7,24). Indeed, conformity to apostolic teaching and submission to apostolic authority were major tests of whether religious teachers really knew and possessed God themselves (1 John 4:6; 2 John 9-10; 3 John 9-10).

The authority of the apostles, which Jesus gave them, and which they self-consciously exercised, was recognized by the early church. The first thing we are

THE AUTHORITY OF THE APOSTLES WAS RECOGNIZED BY THE EARLY CHURCH

told about the newly Spirit-filled church on the day of Pentecost is 'they devoted themselves to the apostles' teaching (Acts 2:42). Spirit-filled churches always do. The post-apostolic fathers understood clearly that the apostles were unique. Clement of Rome wrote to the Corinthians at the end of the first century: 'The apostles received the gospel for us from the Lord Jesus Christ. Jesus Christ was sent forth from God. So then Christ is from God, and the apostles are from Christ.'

At the beginning of the second century, Ignatius, Bishop of Antioch, wrote to the Romans: 'I do not, as Peter and Paul, issue commandments to you [see Acts 4]. They were apostles; I am but a condemned man.'[8] Somewhat later, about AD 200, Tertullian of North Africa was yet more explicit: 'We Christians are forbidden to introduce anything on our own authority or to choose what someone else introduces on his own authority. Our authorities are the Lord's apostles and they in their turn choose to introduce nothing on their own authority. They faithfully passed on to the nations the teaching which they had received from Christ.'[9]

---

8. Ignatius writing to the churches in Tralles and in Magnesia, on his way to his execution in Rome. Trallians, Chapter 3: Magnesians Chapter 13. See also Ephesians 3.

CHOOSING WHAT TO INCLUDE IN THE NEW TESTAMENT

When the time came to settle the canon of the New Testament, and in particular which books should be excluded, the supreme question about every questionable book was whether it possessed apostolic authority. Had it been written by an apostle? If not, did it carry the imprimatur of apostles, in that it came from their circle and represented their teaching? The test of canonicity was apostolicity.

It is tragic in our day to witness the loss of this understanding. People talk of Paul, Peter, John and the other apostles as if they were foolish and gullible first-century Christians whose teaching was nothing more than their own opinions, which could be set aside if we do not like it. Even biblical scholars can be irresponsible

PEOPLE TALK OF THE APOSTLES AS IF THEY WERE FOOLISH AND GULLIBLE

in their treatment of the apostles. 'That's Paul's view', they say, 'or Peter's or John's. But this is mine. And my view is just as good as theirs, in fact better.' But no, the teaching of the apostles is the teaching of Christ. To receive it is to receive Christ; to reject it is to reject Christ.

We need to return to the clear-sighted understanding of the sixteenth century Reformers on this matter! Here, for example, is Luther:

---

9. Tertullian: *Prescriptions against Heretics*, Chapter 6

'Jesus... subjects the whole world to the apostles, through whom alone it should and must be enlightened. All the people in the world – kings, princes, lords, learned men, wise men, holy men — have to sit down while the apostles stand up, have to let themselves be accused and condemned in their wisdom and sanctity as men who know neither doctrine, nor life, nor the right relation to God.'[10]

SUMMARISING THE ARGUMENT

We are ready now to summarize the argument for our acceptance of the whole Bible as God's Word written, uniquely revealed, verbally inspired, supremely authoritative.

THE ARGUMENT IS EASY TO GRASP, AND IMPOSSIBLE TO REFUTE

The argument is easy to grasp, and I think impossible to refute. It centres on the teaching of the Lord Jesus Christ. He endorsed the Old Testament Scriptures, and he made provision for the writing of the New Testament Scriptures

This argument is not circular, as some objectors maintain. They wrongly represent us as saying something like this: 'We know Scripture is inspired because the divine Lord Jesus said so, and we know the Lord Jesus is divine because the inspired Scripture says so.' If that were our position, we would indeed be arguing in a circle.

10. Martin Luther: *Luther's Works*, vol 21, Concordia, 1956, p61.

But our critics mistake our reasoning. Our argument is not circular, but linear. We do not begin by assuming the very inspiration of Scripture which we are setting out to prove. On the contrary, we come to the Gospels (which tell the story of Jesus) without any doctrine of Scripture or theory of inspiration. We are content merely to take them at their face value as first-century historical documents, recording the impressions of eyewitnesses. Next, as we read the Gospels, their testimony through the work of the Holy Spirit leads us to faith in Jesus as Lord. And then this Lord Jesus, in whom we have come to believe, gives us a doctrine of Scripture (his own doctrine) which we did not have at the beginning. Thus the argument runs not in a circle (Scripture witnesses to Jesus who witnesses to Scripture) but in a line (historical documents evoke our faith in Jesus, who then gives us a doctrine of Scripture).

The central issue relates, then, not to the Bible's authority, but to Christ's. If *he* accepted the Old Testament as God's Word, are we going to reject it? If *he* appointed and authorized his apostles, saying to them 'he who receives you receives me,' are we going to reject them? To reject the authority of either the Old Testament or the New Testament is to reject the authority of Christ. It is supremely because we are determined to submit to the authority of Jesus Christ as Lord that we submit to the authority of Scripture.

DOES IT MATTER ANYWAY?

An objector may ask, 'Does it really matter whether the Bible is completely and infallibly true or not? Isn't the argument rather academic and remote from real life?' No. The question of biblical authority is of immense personal, practical and contemporary relevance. Let me show you how vital it is to every Christian's everyday Christianity. I do so through using four deductions.

THE QUESTION OF BIBLICAL AUTHORITY IS OF IMMENSE RELEVANCE

First, submission to the authority of Scripture is critical to Christian discipleship.

That is not to say it is impossible for those who deny the authority of Scripture to be a disciple of Jesus in some sense. There are followers of Jesus whose confidence in Scripture is minimal. But their Christian discipleship is bound to be impaired.

True discipleship includes (a) worship, (b) faith, (c) obedience and (d) hope. Yet each of these is impossible without a reliable, objective revelation from God. Let's focus on each in turn.

(a) *How can we worship God if we do not know his character?* Christians do not worship 'an unknown God' as did the Athenians; we worship 'in truth', as Jesus said we must (John 4:24), and we glory in God's 'name', in his revealed character.

(b) *How can we trust God if we do not know his faithfulness?* Genuine faith is never irrational. It rests on the reliability of a God who has spoken. The foundation of trust is truth – God's truth and truthfulness.

(c) *How can we obey God if we do not know his will?* Obedience is impossible if no laws or commandments have been given us to obey.

(d) *How can we hope in God if we do not know his promises?* Christian hope is not the same as secular optimism. Rather, it is a joyful confidence about the future, which is aroused by and rests on specific promises about the return of Christ and the triumph of God.

Thus worship, faith, obedience and hope – four basic ingredients of Christian discipleship – depend on our knowledge of God. Worship depends on knowing his character; trust depends on knowing his faithfulness; obedience on accepting his commandments; and hope on knowing his promises. And God's character, faithfulness, commandments and promises are all revealed in Scripture. Therefore, Scripture is essential to Christian discipleship. If we want to grow up into maturity as followers of Jesus, the Word of God will be central in our lives.

Second, submission to the authority of Scripture is basic to Christian integrity.

Many deny this and would even affirm the contrary. They regard the acceptance of biblical infallibility as untenable, and charge Christians who hold it with a lack of mental integrity, with intellectual obscurantism, intellectual schizophrenia or intellectual suicide.

But we plead 'not guilty' to these charges and insist that our conviction about Scripture arises from the very integrity which our critics say we lack. For what is integrity? *Integrity* is the quality of an 'integrated' person who is at peace and not at war within himself. Instead of a dichotomy between various beliefs, or between belief and behaviour, there is harmony.

One of the critical and most integrating of all Christian beliefs is the truth that 'Jesus is Lord' (for example: Romans 10:9; 1 Corinthians 12:3; Philippians 2:11). A Christian not only confesses with his lips that Jesus is Lord, but brings every aspect of his life under the sovereign lordship of Jesus – his opinions, his beliefs, his standards, his values, his ambitions, *everything*!

To us, then, submission to Scripture is bound up with submission to the lordship of Jesus. There is no selective submission – for example, agreeing with Jesus in his doctrine of God but disagreeing with him in his doctrine of Scripture; or obeying his command to love our neighbour but disobeying his command

SELECTIVE SUBMISSION IS NOT TRUE SUBMISSION

to make disciples. Selective submission is not true submission. There is in it a reprehensible element of pride and self-will. This is why Paul refers to false teachers (who presume not to 'agree with the sound words of our Lord Jesus Christ') as 'puffed up with conceit' and even as 'insubordinate', an adjective he has just used of unruly children (1 Timothy 6:3-4; Titus 1:6, 10). There is about false (unbiblical) teaching a certain immaturity, arrogance and lack of discipline which arise from an unwillingness to submit our minds to the lordship of Christ.

This principle indicates what we should do with biblical problems. In affirming the full inspiration and authority of Scripture, we are not denying that there are problems – philosophical, scientific, historical, literary and moral. But every Christian doctrine has problems. And we must learn to deal with problems over Scripture exactly as we deal with problems over any other Christian doctrine.

The example I like to give is our belief that 'God is love,' for this is a foundational part of the Christian creed shared by all Christians of all persuasions. Yet the problems surrounding the doctrine are immense – questions about the origin and continuance of evil, about why the innocent suffer, about the so-called 'silences of God' (for example, in unanswered prayers) and the so-called 'acts of God' (that is, natural disasters). What do we do when confronted with such problems? Do we conclude that in order to preserve our intellectual integrity we have to renounce our belief in the love of God? Not at all. We retain our conviction about God's love *in spite of the problems* for the simple and straightforward reason that this is what Jesus taught by word and deed. It is loyalty to Jesus which gives us the true principle of integrity.

It is the same with biblical problems. Of course we should grapple with them. It is no part of Christian responsibility either to pretend they are not there or to ignore them. And as we study them, some will diminish in size or even disappear (many problems which troubled former generations are no longer problems today). Yet some problems will remain. We have to be prepared to live with them, believing that if we had further knowledge, they too would be solved. We certainly should not allow the problems to shift us from our conviction regarding Scripture.

For our view of Scripture depends on our loyalty to Christ, not on our ability to solve all the problems. As with the love of God, so with the Word of God: We hold this doctrine *in spite of the problems* for the simple and straightforward

OUR VIEW OF SCRIPTURE DEPENDS ON OUR LOYALTY TO CHRIST

reason that Jesus taught it and exhibited it. And to believe a Christian doctrine because of the acknowledged lordship of Jesus Christ cannot possibly be dismissed as obscurantism. It is the very opposite. It is Christian humility, Christian sobriety, Christian integrity.

Third, submission to the authority of Scripture is essential to Christian freedom.

Once again, many imagine the reverse to be true. I have several times used the word *submission* – submission to the authority of Scripture and submission to the lordship of Christ. And to large numbers of our contemporaries, *submission* and *freedom* are incompatible. If I am to be free, they say, I must rebel against all authority; to submit to any rule (whether intellectual or moral) is to lose my freedom. But those who say such things have not yet grasped the character of true freedom.

True freedom is not absolute. Intellectual freedom, for example, is not the same as free thought. What do you say of the flat-earther who denies that the earth is round? Is he free? Not at all. He is a fool. He is also a prisoner, in bondage to falsehood and fantasy. Again, what do you say of a man who denies the law of gravity and jumps from the top of a New York skyscraper, or from the Shanghai Tower. His 'freedom' becomes a synonym for suicide.

True intellectual freedom is found not in independence of the truth, but in submission to the truth, whether the truth is scientific or biblical. When the mind submits to the truth, it is set free from falsehood, from the human deceits and the devil's lies, from its own subjective insecurity, from the shifting sands of existential experience, and from the ever-changing fashions of the world. Submission to truth is the true freedom.

> *TRUE INTELLECTUAL FREEDOM IS FOUND IN SUBMISSION TO TRUTH*

Jesus himself taught this. He said that whoever commits sin is the slave of sin, and that, in contrast to this bondage, he could set us free. What was the freedom which he promised? 'If you continue in my word, you are truly my disciples, and you will know the truth, and the truth will make you free' (John 8:31,36). Freedom is found in discipleship, and discipleship is continuing submission to the Word of Jesus, for the Word of Jesus is the truth. No wonder Paul wrote of his resolve to take every thought captive to obey Christ' (2 Corinthians 10:5).

Fourth, submission to the authority of Scripture is essential to Christian witness.

The contemporary world is in great confusion and darkness. Human hearts are failing for fear. Has the Christian church any word of assurance for our bewilderment, any light for our darkness, any hope for our fear? One of the greatest tragedies of today is

THE CHURCH IS BECOMING LESS SURE OF ITS MISSION

that just when the world is becoming more aware of its need, the church is becoming less sure of its mission. And the major reason for the diminishing Christian mission is diminishing confidence in the Christian message.

We Christians should affirm with great confidence that Jesus is the supreme Lord, to whom all authority has been given in heaven and on earth, and that he bids us go and make disciples and teach them all his teaching (Matthew 28:18 19). His commission is to proclaim his name as the crucified and risen Saviour. For only in his name will forgiveness and new life be available to all who repent and believe (Luke 24:44-49).

We have no liberty to alter these terms of reference which Christ gave his church in his commission. There is only one gospel. We may neither embellish nor modify nor manipulate it. We are to be the heralds of God's good news. We are charged to lift up our voice with strength, to lift it up without fear and

WE HAVE NO LIBERTY TO ALTER THESE TERMS OF REFERENCE

to publish abroad the salvation of God. (Isaiah 40:9; 52:7). Our announcement is given to us; we do not invent it. All we contribute is the voice to make it known, yes, and the life and love which lie behind the voice. In this respect every Christian resembles John the Baptist. For each of us is to be but a voice crying in the world's dry wilderness, bearing witness to Christ, gladly decreasing in ourselves in order that he may increase (Mark 1:2-3; John 1:6-8, 19-23; 3:30).

TO CONCLUDE

I have tried to develop two great themes about submission to the authority of Scripture. *First*, that submission to Scripture cannot be separated from acknowledging the lordship of Jesus. *Second*, that submission to Scripture is the basis of everyday Christian living, for without it Christian discipleship,

Christian integrity, Christian freedom and Christian witness are all seriously damaged, if not destroyed.

Christ still calls us to take his yoke upon us and learn from him (assuming his yoke is a metaphor for submitting to his teaching authority). He still promises that under his yoke we shall find rest for our souls; and he still assures us that he himself is gentle, and that (unlike all other yokes) his yoke is easy and *his* burden is light (Matthew 11:29-30).

Put these to the test. If you do, you will find them, as I have, to be true.

John Stott (1921-2011), pastor-theologian, university evangelist, and author of over 50 books, served as Rector then Rector Emeritus of All Souls Church, Langham Place, London. He founded EFAC (Evangelical Fellowship in the Anglican Communion), Langham Partnership, and LICC (London Institute for Contemporary Christianity).

PART 2

JOY IN THE BIBLE

JOY IN THE BIBLE

Authority and joy are words which are rarely paired, yet in the Christian life they cannot be separated. In the Foreword, Don Cormack has traced the thread between authority, self-discipline, grace and joy, noting how McCheyne wanted his reading plan to be a means of bringing joy.

So now we turn to joy in the Bible. Sinclair Ferguson's article first appeared in Table Talk *magazine in 2017. We publish it here with the full text of the Scriptures he refers to.*

While shaking hands at the church door, ministers are sometimes greeted with a spontaneous, 'I really enjoyed that!'— which is immediately followed by, 'Oh! I shouldn't really say that, should I?' I usually grip tighter, hold the handshake a little longer, and say with a smile, 'Doesn't the catechism's first question encourage us to do that?[11] If we are to enjoy him forever, why not begin now?'

Of course, we cannot enjoy God apart from glorifying him. And the *Westminster Shorter Catechism* wisely goes on to ask, 'What rule hath God given to

---

11. The Westminster Shorter Catechism (1647), designed to teach Christian doctrine in a Q & A form, begins with the question 'What is man's chief end?' And its answer: 'Man's chief end is to glorify God and to enjoy him forever.'

direct us how we may glorify and enjoy him?' But notice that Scripture contains the 'rule' for enjoying God as well as glorifying him. We know it abounds in instructions for glorifying him, but how does it instruct us to 'enjoy him'?

NOTICE THAT SCRIPTURE CONTAINS THE 'RULE' FOR ENJOYING GOD

Enjoying God is a command, not an optional extra: 'Rejoice in the Lord always; again I will say, rejoice' (Philippians 4:4). But how? We cannot 'rejoice to order,' can we?

True. Yet, Scripture shows that well-instructed believers develop a determination to rejoice. They *will* rejoice in the Lord. The prophet Habakkuk exemplified this in difficult days:

> Though the fig tree does not bud
> and there are no grapes on the vines,
> though the olive crop fails
> and the fields produce no food,
> though there are no sheep in the pen
> and no cattle in the stalls,
> yet I will rejoice in the Lord,
> I will be joyful in God my Saviour.
> (Habakkuk 3:17,18)

The prophet exercised what our forefathers called 'acting faith' – a vigorous determination to experience whatever the Lord commands, including joy, and to use the God-given means to do so. Here are four of these means – in which, it should be noted, we also glorify God.

Scripture shows that well-instructed believers develop a determination to rejoice.

JOY IN SALVATION
Enjoying God means relishing the salvation he gives us in Jesus Christ. 'I will take joy in the God of my salvation' (Habakkuk 3:18). God takes joy in our salvation. So should we.

We see examples of this in the following parables:

The lost sheep: Then he calls his friends and neighbours together and says, 'Rejoice with me; I have found my sheep.' I tell you that in the same way there will be more rejoicing in heaven over one sinner who repents than over ninety-nine righteous persons who do not need to repent. (Luke 15:6-7)

The lost coin: And when she finds it, she calls her friends and neighbours together and says, 'Rejoice with me; I have found my lost coin.' In the same way, I tell you, there is rejoicing in the presence of the angels of God over one sinner who repents. (Luke 15:9-10)

The lost son: The father said, '... we had to celebrate and be glad, because this brother of yours was dead and is alive again; he was lost and is found. (Luke 15:32)

In Ephesians 1, the Apostle Paul provides a masterly delineation of salvation in Christ. It is a gospel bath in which we should often luxuriate, and rungs on a ladder we should frequently climb, in order to experience the joy of the Lord as our strength. (Nehemiah 8:10)

> Praise be to the God and Father of our Lord Jesus Christ, who has blessed us in the heavenly realms with every spiritual blessing in Christ. For he chose us in him before the creation of the world to be holy and blameless in his sight. In love he predestined us for adoption to sonship through Jesus Christ, in accordance with his pleasure and will— to the praise of his glorious grace, which he has freely given us in the One he loves. In him we have redemption through his blood, the forgiveness of sins, in accordance with the riches of God's grace that he lavished on us. With all wisdom and understanding, he made known to us the mystery of his will according to his good pleasure, which he purposed in Christ, to be put into effect when the times reach their fulfilment—to bring unity to all things in heaven and on earth under Christ.

> In him we were also chosen, having been predestined according to the plan of him who works out everything in conformity with

the purpose of his will, in order that we, who
were the first to put our hope in Christ, might
be for the praise of his glory. And you also
were included in Christ when you heard the
message of truth, the gospel of your salvation.
When you believed, you were marked in him
with a seal, the promised Holy Spirit, who is a
deposit guaranteeing our inheritance until the
redemption of those who are God's possession—
to the praise of his glory. (Ephesians 1:3-14)

While we are commanded to have joy, the resources
to do so are outside of ourselves, known only through
union with Christ.

JOY IN REVELATION
Joy issues from devouring inscripturated revelation.
Psalm 119 bears repeated witness to this, as we see
here. The psalmist 'delights' in God's testimonies 'as
much as in all riches':

I rejoice in following your statutes
as one rejoices in great riches.

Direct me in the path of your commands,
for there I find delight.

I will speak of your statutes before kings
and I will not be put to shame,
for I delight in your commands
because I love them.

Their hearts are callous and unfeeling,
but I delight in your law.

Let your compassion come to me that I may live,
for your law is my delight.

How sweet are your words to my taste,
sweeter than honey to my mouth.
I rejoice in your promise
like one who finds great spoil.

I long for your salvation, O Lord
and your law is my delight.
(Psalm 119:14, 35, 46, 47, 70, 77, 103, 162, 174)

Think of Jesus' words, 'These things I have spoken to you, that my joy may be in you, and that your joy may be full' (John 15:11).

Does he mean he will find his joy in us, so that our joy may be full; or that his joy will be in us so that our joy may be full? Both, surely, are true. We find full joy in the Lord only when we know he finds his joy in us. The pathway to joy, then, is to give ourselves maximum exposure to his Word and to let it dwell in us richly.

Let the word of Christ dwell in you richly as you teach and admonish one another with all wisdom, and as you sing psalms, hymns, and spiritual songs with gratitude in your hearts to God. (Colossians 3:16)

The Bible is joy-food for the joy-hungry soul.

JOY IN COMMUNION

There is joy in the Lord to be tasted in the worship we enjoy in church communion. The church is the new Jerusalem, the city that cannot be hidden,

> It is beautiful in its loftiness,
> The joy of the whole earth. (Psalm 48:2)

In the Spirit-led communion of praise and petition; in pastoring the flock; in preaching the Word; in singing psalms, hymns, and spiritual songs; and in the receiving of water, bread, and wine, abundant joy is to be found.

> The Lord your God is with you,
> he is mighty to save.
> He will take great delight in you,
> he will quiet you with his love,
> he will rejoice over you with singing.
> (Zephaniah 3:17)

The Lord sings over us with joy. Our hearts sing for joy in return.

JOY IN TRIBULATION

Here, indeed, is a divine paradox. There is joy to be known in the midst of and through affliction. Viewed biblically, tribulation is the Father's chastising hand using life's pain and darkness to mould us into the image of the One who endured for the sake of the joy set before him. From Hebrews 12:1-11:

> Therefore, since we are surrounded by such a great cloud of witnesses, let us throw off everything that hinders and the sin that so easily entangles. And let us run with perseverance the race marked out for us, fixing our eyes on Jesus, the pioneer and perfecter of faith. For the joy set before him he endured the cross, scorning its shame, and sat down at the right hand of the throne of God.

> And have you completely forgotten this word of encouragement that addresses you as a father addresses his son? It says,

> 'My son, do not make light of the Lord's discipline,
>   and do not lose heart when he rebukes you,
> because the Lord disciplines the one he loves,
>   and he chastens everyone he accepts as his son.'

> Endure hardship as discipline; God is treating you as his children. For what children are not disciplined by their father? If you are not disciplined—and everyone undergoes discipline—then you are not legitimate, not true sons and daughters at all. Moreover, we have all had human fathers who disciplined us and we respected them for it. How much more should we submit to the Father of spirits and live! They

disciplined us for a little while as they thought
best; but God disciplines us for our good, in order
that we may share in his holiness. No discipline
seems pleasant at the time, but painful. Later on,
however, it produces a harvest of righteousness
and peace for those who have been trained by it.

For those God foreknew he also predestined to
be conformed to the likeness of his Son, that he
might be the firstborn among many brothers.
(Romans 8:29)

We exult and rejoice in our sufferings, Paul says,
because 'suffering produces . . . hope' in us. And we
boast in the hope of the glory of God.

Not only so, but we also glory in our sufferings,
because we know that suffering produces
perseverance; perseverance, character; and
character, hope. (Romans 5:3-4)

Peter and James echo the same principle:

Praise be to the God and Father of our Lord
Jesus Christ! In his great mercy he has given
us new birth into a living hope through the
resurrection of Jesus Christ from the dead, and
into an inheritance that can never perish, spoil
or fade. This inheritance is kept in heaven for
you, who through faith are shielded by God's
power until the coming of the salvation that is

ready to be revealed in the last time. In all this you greatly rejoice, though now for a little while you may have had to suffer grief in all kinds of trials. These have come so that the proven genuineness of your faith—of greater worth than gold, which perishes even though refined by fire—may result in praise, glory and honour when Jesus Christ is revealed. Though you have not seen him, you love him; and even though you do not see him now, you believe in him and are filled with an inexpressible and glorious joy, for you are receiving the end result of your faith, the salvation of your souls. (l Peter 1:3-8)

Consider it pure joy, my brothers and sisters, whenever you face trials of many kinds, because you know that the testing of your faith produces perseverance. Let perseverance finish its work so that you may be mature and complete, not lacking anything. (James 1:2-4)

The knowledge of the sure hand of God in providence not only brings stability; it also produces joy.

All of this adds up to exultation in God himself. In Romans 5, Paul leads us from rejoicing in the hope of the glory of God (v2) to joy that comes in tribulation (v3) to exulting in God himself (v11).

Therefore, since we have been justified through faith, we have peace with God through our Lord Jesus Christ, through whom we have gained access by faith into this grace in which we now stand. And we boast in the hope of the glory of God. Not only so, but we also glory in our sufferings, because we know that suffering produces perseverance; perseverance, character; and character, hope. And hope does not put us to shame, because God's love has been poured out into our hearts through the Holy Spirit, who has been given to us.

You see, at just the right time, when we were still powerless, Christ died for the ungodly. Very rarely will anyone die for a righteous person, though for a good person someone might possibly dare to die. But God demonstrates his own love for us in this: While we were still sinners, Christ died for us.

Since we have now been justified by his blood, how much more shall we be saved from God's wrath through him! For if, while we were God's enemies, we were reconciled to him through the death of his Son, how much more, having been reconciled, shall we be saved through his life! Not only is this so, but we also boast in God through our Lord Jesus Christ, through whom we have now received reconciliation. (Romans 5:1-11)

Then I will go to the altar of God,
To God, my joy and my delight.
I will praise you with the harp, O God, my God.
(Psalm 43:4)

The unbeliever can't imagine this, because he has been blinded by the joy-depriving lie of Satan that to glorify God is the high road to joylessness. Thankfully, Christ reveals that in him the reverse takes place— because of our salvation, through his revelation, in worship's blessed communion, and by means of tribulation.

Enjoy! Yes, indeed. And in the words of the prophet Isaiah, may 'everlasting joy . . . be upon [your] heads' (Isaiah 51:11).

Sinclair Ferguson, pastor-theologian and author, has pastored churches in the Shetland Isles and Glasgow; and in Columbia, South Carolina. He has held chairs in Systematic Theology at Westminster Seminary, Philadelphia; Redeemer Seminary, Dallas; and Reformed Theological Seminary; and served as Teaching Fellow of Ligonier Ministries. He is an elder of St Peter's Free Church, Dundee.

FOR REFLECTION

The story of Pastor Hom and his bedraggled group (p xii) illustrates the true reality of Authority and Joy. Let us be humbled anew by the lives of those 'of whom the world is not worthy'.

'We believe in Jesus and we believe Jesus' (p7). We readily give assent to the first half of this statement, but we may find the second half arresting. Let's reflect on what it would mean to renew this belief, in our prayers, and in our Bible reading.

John Stott's arguments for the authority of the Old and New Testaments, and for why this authority matters, are worth reviewing, so we can use them in helping or reasoning with others: whether Christians or those who don't believe.

We must not lose sight of Joy in the Bible, and what it means to enjoy God. You may like to take each section of Part ll and reflect on Joy in Salvation; Joy in Revelation; Joy in Communion; and Joy in Tribulation.

Hear again Jesus's words spoken to his disciples on the night he was betrayed: 'These things I have spoken to you, that my joy may be in you, and that your joy may be full' (John 15:11).

PART 3

McCHEYNE BIBLE
READING PLAN

INTRODUCTION

This reading plan will take you through the New Testament and Psalms twice, and the rest of the Bible once each year. To use it over two years, choose the readings on only one side of the page.

Robert Murray McCheyne drew up the plan for his own congregation in St Peter's Free Church, Dundee. He wanted his church members to get a feel for the sweep of salvation history. He also wanted their Bible reading to be a source of joy, not a burden. The plan, first used in Dundee in 1843, is now used by thousands across the world.

This is what McCheyne wrote to his congregation to introduce the plan. The language sounds archaic, but we leave it as it was penned.

> *Some may engage in reading with alacrity for a time, and afterwards feel it a burden grievous to be borne. They may find their conscience dragging them through the appointed task without any relish of the heavenly food. If this be the case with any, throw aside the fetter, and feed at liberty in the sweet garden of God. My desire is not to cast a snare on you, but to be a helper of your joy.*

30 December 1842

TO START YOU OFF

The late Dr Martyn Lloyd-Jones introduced me to the McCheyne calendar in the 1950s, and I have used it ever since. To me its great value is that it begins with the four 'great beginnings' in Scripture–Genesis (the birth of the universe), Ezra (the rebirth of the nation after Babylonian captivity), Matthew (the birth of Christ) and Acts (the birth of the body of Christ). Then we follow the unfolding of these four stories. Nothing has helped me more than this to grasp the grand themes of the Bible.

John Stott (1921-2011) *Globally-renowned pastor-theologian. Founder of Langham Partnership and EFAC*

Why not use this with a few friends? You can talk about what you've read and keep one another going! I try to understand what I'm reading much more if I know I'm going to have a conversation about it later.

Elaine Duncan *Chief Executive, Scottish Bible Society*

For those whose lifestyle is organized, this system is a great asset, while for those whose lifestyle is more chaotic, it pulls us back into line. Reading the Bible is a tough discipline, and we all fail at times, but do press on and don't be defeated.

Phillip Jensen *Former Dean of Sydney*

I find that some sections of Scripture which seem to be the least exciting are the ones which speak to areas of greatest need in my spiritual life. So I need to make sure I regularly read the whole Bible. In this way, 'the whole counsel of God' is able to challenge my mind, which is so prone to straying from God's way of thinking.

Ajith Fernando *Teaching Director, Sri Lanka Youth for Christ*

The world is constantly clamouring for our minds, and this is why I warmly encourage you to make use of the McCheyne Bible Reading Plan. It anchors hearts in the Word of God.

Joni Eareckson Tada *President, Joni and Friends*

McCheyne's Bible reading plan has been the mainstay of my private devotions for over 25 years. I cannot recommend it highly enough. I read one chapter four times a day. As a result of this limited investment of time, I read the whole Bible through every year. This has provided milk, meat, honey and dynamite for my soul, and for the whole basis of my ministry. Use it and see!

David Robertson *McCheyne biographer, and former minister of St Peter's Free Church, Dundee (1992-2019)*

1	Genesis 1	Matthew 1	☐
2	Genesis 2	Matthew 2	☐
3	Genesis 3	Matthew 3	☐
4	Genesis 4	Matthew 4	☐
5	Genesis 5	Matthew 5	☐
6	Genesis 6	Matthew 6	☐
7	Genesis 7	Matthew 7	☐
8	Genesis 8	Matthew 8	☐
9	Genesis 9-10	Matthew 9	☐
10	Genesis 11	Matthew 10	☐
11	Genesis 12	Matthew 11	☐
12	Genesis 13	Matthew 12	☐
13	Genesis 14	Matthew 13	☐
14	Genesis 15	Matthew 14	☐
15	Genesis 16	Matthew 15	☐
16	Genesis 17	Matthew 16	☐
17	Genesis 18	Matthew 17	☐
18	Genesis 19	Matthew 18	☐
19	Genesis 20	Matthew 19	☐
20	Genesis 21	Matthew 20	☐
21	Genesis 22	Matthew 21	☐
22	Genesis 23	Matthew 22	☐
23	Genesis 24	Matthew 23	☐
24	Genesis 25	Matthew 24	☐
25	Genesis 26	Matthew 25	☐
26	Genesis 27	Matthew 26	☐
27	Genesis 28	Matthew 27	☐
28	Genesis 29	Matthew 28	☐
29	Genesis 30	Mark 1	☐
30	Genesis 31	Mark 2	☐
31	Genesis 32	Mark 3	☐

Ezra 1	Acts 1	☐
Ezra 2	Acts 2	☐
Ezra 3	Acts 3	☐
Ezra 4	Acts 4	☐
Ezra 5	Acts 5	☐
Ezra 6	Acts 6	☐
Ezra 7	Acts 7	☐
Ezra 8	Acts 8	☐
Ezra 9	Acts 9	☐
Ezra 10	Acts 10	☐
Nehemiah 1	Acts 11	☐
Nehemiah 2	Acts 12	☐
Nehemiah 3	Acts 13	☐
Nehemiah 4	Acts 14	☐
Nehemiah 5	Acts 15	☐
Nehemiah 6	Acts 16	☐
Nehemiah 7	Acts 17	☐
Nehemiah 8	Acts 18	☐
Nehemiah 9	Acts 19	☐
Nehemiah 10	Acts 20	☐
Nehemiah 11	Acts 21	☐
Nehemiah 12	Acts 22	☐
Nehemiah 13	Acts 23	☐
Esther 1	Acts 24	☐
Esther 2	Acts 25	☐
Esther 3	Acts 26	☐
Esther 4	Acts 27	☐
Esther 5	Acts 28	☐
Esther 6	Romans 1	☐
Esther 7	Romans 2	☐
Esther 8	Romans 3	☐

1	Genesis 33	Mark 4	☐
2	Genesis 34	Mark 5	☐
3	Genesis 35-36	Mark 6	☐
4	Genesis 37	Mark 7	☐
5	Genesis 38	Mark 8	☐
6	Genesis 39	Mark 9	☐
7	Genesis 40	Mark 10	☐
8	Genesis 41	Mark 11	☐
9	Genesis 42	Mark 12	☐
10	Genesis 43	Mark 13	☐
11	Genesis 44	Mark 14	☐
12	Genesis 45	Mark 15	☐
13	Genesis 46	Mark 16	☐
14	Genesis 47	Luke 1:1-38	☐
15	Genesis 48	Luke 1:39-80	☐
16	Genesis 49	Luke 2	☐
17	Genesis 50	Luke 3	☐
18	Exodus 1	Luke 4	☐
19	Exodus 2	Luke 5	☐
20	Exodus 3	Luke 6	☐
21	Exodus 4	Luke 7	☐
22	Exodus 5	Luke 8	☐
23	Exodus 6	Luke 9	☐
24	Exodus 7	Luke 10	☐
25	Exodus 8	Luke 11	☐
26	Exodus 9	Luke 12	☐
27	Exodus 10	Luke 13	☐
28	Exodus 11-12:20	Luke 14	☐

Esther 9-10	Romans 4	☐
Job 1	Romans 5	☐
Job 2	Romans 6	☐
Job 3	Romans 7	☐
Job 4	Romans 8	☐
Job 5	Romans 9	☐
Job 6	Romans 10	☐
Job 7	Romans 11	☐
Job 8	Romans 12	☐
Job 9	Romans 13	☐
Job 10	Romans 14	☐
Job 11	Romans 15	☐
Job 12	Romans 16	☐
Job 13	1 Corinthians 1	☐
Job 14	1 Corinthians 2	☐
Job 15	1 Corinthians 3	☐
Job 16-17	1 Corinthians 4	☐
Job 18	1 Corinthians 5	☐
Job 19	1 Corinthians 6	☐
Job 20	1 Corinthians 7	☐
Job 21	1 Corinthians 8	☐
Job 22	1 Corinthians 9	☐
Job 23	1 Corinthians 10	☐
Job 24	1 Corinthians 11	☐
Job 25-26	1 Corinthians 12	☐
Job 27	1 Corinthians 13	☐
Job 28	1 Corinthians 14	☐
Job 29	1 Corinthians 15	☐

1	Exodus 12:21-51	Luke 15	☐
2	Exodus 13	Luke 16	☐
3	Exodus 14	Luke 17	☐
4	Exodus 15	Luke 18	☐
5	Exodus 16	Luke 19	☐
6	Exodus 17	Luke 20	☐
7	Exodus 18	Luke 21	☐
8	Exodus 19	Luke 22	☐
9	Exodus 20	Luke 23	☐
10	Exodus 21	Luke 24	☐
11	Exodus 22	John 1	☐
12	Exodus 23	John 2	☐
13	Exodus 24	John 3	☐
14	Exodus 25	John 4	☐
15	Exodus 26	John 5	☐
16	Exodus 27	John 6	☐
17	Exodus 28	John 7	☐
18	Exodus 29	John 8	☐
19	Exodus 30	John 9	☐
20	Exodus 31	John 10	☐
21	Exodus 32	John 11	☐
22	Exodus 33	John 12	☐
23	Exodus 34	John 13	☐
24	Exodus 35	John 14	☐
25	Exodus 36	John 15	☐
26	Exodus 37	John 16	☐
27	Exodus 38	John 17	☐
28	Exodus 39	John 18	☐
29	Exodus 40	John 19	☐
30	Leviticus 1	John 20	☐
31	Leviticus 2-3	John 21	☐

Job 30	1 Corinthians 16	☐
Job 31	2 Corinthians 1	☐
Job 32	2 Corinthians 2	☐
Job 33	2 Corinthians 3	☐
Job 34	2 Corinthians 4	☐
Job 35	2 Corinthians 5	☐
Job 36	2 Corinthians 6	☐
Job 37	2 Corinthians 7	☐
Job 38	2 Corinthians 8	☐
Job 39	2 Corinthians 9	☐
Job 40	2 Corinthians 10	☐
Job 41	2 Corinthians 11	☐
Job 42	2 Corinthians 12	☐
Proverbs 1	2 Corinthians 13	☐
Proverbs 2	Galatians 1	☐
Proverbs 3	Galatians 2	☐
Proverbs 4	Galatians 3	☐
Proverbs 5	Galatians 4	☐
Proverbs 6	Galatians 5	☐
Proverbs 7	Galatians 6	☐
Proverbs 8	Ephesians 1	☐
Proverbs 9	Ephesians 2	☐
Proverbs 10	Ephesians 3	☐
Proverbs 11	Ephesians 4	☐
Proverbs 12	Ephesians 5	☐
Proverbs 13	Ephesians 6	☐
Proverbs 14	Philippians 1	☐
Proverbs 15	Philippians 2	☐
Proverbs 16	Philippians 3	☐
Proverbs 17	Philippians 4	☐
Proverbs 18	Colossians 1	☐

1	Leviticus 4	Psalms 1-2	☐
2	Leviticus 5	Psalms 3-4	☐
3	Leviticus 6	Psalms 5-6	☐
4	Leviticus 7	Psalms 7-8	☐
5	Leviticus 8	Psalm 9	☐
6	Leviticus 9	Psalm 10	☐
7	Leviticus 10	Psalms 11-12	☐
8	Leviticus 11-12	Psalms 13-14	☐
9	Leviticus 13	Psalms 15-16	☐
10	Leviticus 14	Psalm 17	☐
11	Leviticus 15	Psalm 18	☐
12	Leviticus 16	Psalm 19	☐
13	Leviticus 17	Psalms 20-21	☐
14	Leviticus 18	Psalm 22	☐
15	Leviticus 19	Psalms 23-24	☐
16	Leviticus 20	Psalm 25	☐
17	Leviticus 21	Psalms 26-27	☐
18	Leviticus 22	Psalms 28-29	☐
19	Leviticus 23	Psalm 30	☐
20	Leviticus 24	Psalm 31	☐
21	Leviticus 25	Psalm 32	☐
22	Leviticus 26	Psalm 33	☐
23	Leviticus 27	Psalm 34	☐
24	Numbers 1	Psalm 35	☐
25	Numbers 2	Psalm 36	☐
26	Numbers 3	Psalm 37	☐
27	Numbers 4	Psalm 38	☐
28	Numbers 5	Psalm 39	☐
29	Numbers 6	Psalms 40-41	☐
30	Numbers 7	Psalms 42-43	☐

Proverbs 19	Colossians 2	☐
Proverbs 20	Colossians 3	☐
Proverbs 21	Colossians 4	☐
Proverbs 22	1 Thessalonians 1	☐
Proverbs 23	1 Thessalonians 2	☐
Proverbs 24	1 Thessalonians 3	☐
Proverbs 25	1 Thessalonians 4	☐
Proverbs 26	1 Thessalonians 5	☐
Proverbs 27	2 Thessalonians 1	☐
Proverbs 28	2 Thessalonians 2	☐
Proverbs 29	2 Thessalonians 3	☐
Proverbs 30	1 Timothy 1	☐
Proverbs 31	1 Timothy 2	☐
Ecclesiastes 1	1 Timothy 3	☐
Ecclesiastes 2	1 Timothy 4	☐
Ecclesiastes 3	1 Timothy 5	☐
Ecclesiastes 4	1 Timothy 6	☐
Ecclesiastes 5	2 Timothy 1	☐
Ecclesiastes 6	2 Timothy 2	☐
Ecclesiastes 7	2 Timothy 3	☐
Ecclesiastes 8	2 Timothy 4	☐
Ecclesiastes 9	Titus 1	☐
Ecclesiastes 10	Titus 2	☐
Ecclesiastes 11	Titus 3	☐
Ecclesiastes 12	Philemon	☐
Song of Songs 1	Hebrews 1	☐
Song of Songs 2	Hebrews 2	☐
Song of Songs 3	Hebrews 3	☐
Song of Songs 4	Hebrews 4	☐
Song of Songs 5	Hebrews 5	☐

1	Numbers 8	Psalm 44	☐
2	Numbers 9	Psalm 45	☐
3	Numbers 10	Psalms 46-47	☐
4	Numbers 11	Psalm 48	☐
5	Numbers 12-13	Psalm 49	☐
6	Numbers 14	Psalm 50	☐
7	Numbers 15	Psalm 51	☐
8	Numbers 16	Psalms 52-54	☐
9	Numbers 17-18	Psalm 55	☐
10	Numbers 19	Psalms 56-57	☐
11	Numbers 20	Psalm 58-59	☐
12	Numbers 21	Psalms 60-61	☐
13	Numbers 22	Psalms 62-63	☐
14	Numbers 23	Psalms 64-65	☐
15	Numbers 24	Psalms 66-67	☐
16	Numbers 25	Psalm 68	☐
17	Numbers 26	Psalm 69	☐
18	Numbers 27	Psalms 70-71	☐
19	Numbers 28	Psalm 72	☐
20	Numbers 29	Psalm 73	☐
21	Numbers 30	Psalm 74	☐
22	Numbers 31	Psalms 75-76	☐
23	Numbers 32	Psalm 77	☐
24	Numbers 33	Psalm 78:1-39	☐
25	Numbers 34	Psalm 78:40-72	☐
26	Numbers 35	Psalm 79	☐
27	Numbers 36	Psalm 80	☐
28	Deuteronomy 1	Psalms 81-82	☐
29	Deuteronomy 2	Psalms 83-84	☐
30	Deuteronomy 3	Psalm 85	☐
31	Deuteronomy 4	Psalms 86-87	☐

Song of Songs 6	Hebrews 6	☐
Song of Songs 7	Hebrews 7	☐
Song of Songs 8	Hebrews 8	☐
Isaiah 1	Hebrews 9	☐
Isaiah 2	Hebrews 10	☐
Isaiah 3-4	Hebrews 11	☐
Isaiah 5	Hebrews 12	☐
Isaiah 6	Hebrews 13	☐
Isaiah 7	James 1	☐
Isaiah 8-9:7	James 2	☐
Isaiah 9:8-10:4	James 3	☐
Isaiah 10:5-34	James 4	☐
Isaiah 11-12	James 5	☐
Isaiah 13	1 Peter 1	☐
Isaiah 14	1 Peter 2	☐
Isaiah 15	1 Peter 3	☐
Isaiah 16	1 Peter 4	☐
Isaiah 17-18	1 Peter 5	☐
Isaiah 19-20	2 Peter 1	☐
Isaiah 21	2 Peter 2	☐
Isaiah 22	2 Peter 3	☐
Isaiah 23	1 John 1	☐
Isaiah 24	1 John 2	☐
Isaiah 25	1 John 3	☐
Isaiah 26	1 John 4	☐
Isaiah 27	1 John 5	☐
Isaiah 28	2 John	☐
Isaiah 29	3 John	☐
Isaiah 30	Jude	☐
Isaiah 31	Revelation 1	☐
Isaiah 32	Revelation 2	☐

1	Deuteronomy 5	Psalm 88	☐
2	Deuteronomy 6	Psalm 89	☐
3	Deuteronomy 7	Psalm 90	☐
4	Deuteronomy 8	Psalm 91	☐
5	Deuteronomy 9	Psalms 92-93	☐
6	Deuteronomy 10	Psalm 94	☐
7	Deuteronomy 11	Psalms 95-96	☐
8	Deuteronomy 12	Psalms 97-98	☐
9	Deuteronomy 13-14	Psalms 99-101	☐
10	Deuteronomy 15	Psalm 102	☐
11	Deuteronomy 16	Psalm 103	☐
12	Deuteronomy 17	Psalm 104	☐
13	Deuteronomy 18	Psalm 105	☐
14	Deuteronomy 19	Psalm 106	☐
15	Deuteronomy 20	Psalm 107	☐
16	Deuteronomy 21	Psalms 108-109	☐
17	Deuteronomy 22	Psalms 110-111	☐
18	Deuteronomy 23	Psalms 112-113	☐
19	Deuteronomy 24	Psalms 114-115	☐
20	Deuteronomy 25	Psalm 116	☐
21	Deuteronomy 26	Psalms 117-118	☐
22	Deuteronomy 27-28:19	Psalm 119:1-24	☐
23	Deuteronomy 28:20-68	Psalm 119:25-48	☐
24	Deuteronomy 29	Psalm 119:49-72	☐
25	Deuteronomy 30	Psalm 119:73-96	☐
26	Deuteronomy 31	Psalm 119:97-120	☐
27	Deuteronomy 32	Psalm 119:121-144	☐
28	Deuteronomy 33-34	Psalm 119:145-176	☐
29	Joshua 1	Psalms 120-122	☐
30	Joshua 2	Psalms 123-125	☐

Isaiah 33	Revelation 3	☐
Isaiah 34	Revelation 4	☐
Isaiah 35	Revelation 5	☐
Isaiah 36	Revelation 6	☐
Isaiah 37	Revelation 7	☐
Isaiah 38	Revelation 8	☐
Isaiah 39	Revelation 9	☐
Isaiah 40	Revelation 10	☐
Isaiah 41	Revelation 11	☐
Isaiah 42	Revelation 12	☐
Isaiah 43	Revelation 13	☐
Isaiah 44	Revelation 14	☐
Isaiah 45	Revelation 15	☐
Isaiah 46	Revelation 16	☐
Isaiah 47	Revelation 17	☐
Isaiah 48	Revelation 18	☐
Isaiah 49	Revelation 19	☐
Isaiah 50	Revelation 20	☐
Isaiah 51	Revelation 21	☐
Isaiah 52	Revelation 22	☐
Isaiah 53	Matthew 1	☐
Isaiah 54	Matthew 2	☐
Isaiah 55	Matthew 3	☐
Isaiah 56	Matthew 4	☐
Isaiah 57	Matthew 5	☐
Isaiah 58	Matthew 6	☐
Isaiah 59	Matthew 7	☐
Isaiah 60	Matthew 8	☐
Isaiah 61	Matthew 9	☐
Isaiah 62	Matthew 10	☐

1	Joshua 3	Psalms 126-128	☐
2	Joshua 4	Psalms 129-131	☐
3	Joshua 5	Psalms 132-134	☐
4	Joshua 6	Psalms 135-136	☐
5	Joshua 7	Psalms 137-138	☐
6	Joshua 8	Psalm 139	☐
7	Joshua 9	Psalms 140-141	☐
8	Joshua 10	Psalms 142-143	☐
9	Joshua 11	Psalm 144	☐
10	Joshua 12-13	Psalm 145	☐
11	Joshua 14-15	Psalms 146-147	☐
12	Joshua 16-17	Psalm 148	☐
13	Joshua 18-19	Psalms 149-150	☐
14	Joshua 20-21	Acts 1	☐
15	Joshua 22	Acts 2	☐
16	Joshua 23	Acts 3	☐
17	Joshua 24	Acts 4	☐
18	Judges 1	Acts 5	☐
19	Judges 2	Acts 6	☐
20	Judges 3	Acts 7	☐
21	Judges 4	Acts 8	☐
22	Judges 5	Acts 9	☐
23	Judges 6	Acts 10	☐
24	Judges 7	Acts 11	☐
25	Judges 8	Acts 12	☐
26	Judges 9	Acts 13	☐
27	Judges 10	Acts 14	☐
28	Judges 11	Acts 15	☐
29	Judges 12	Acts 16	☐
30	Judges 13	Acts 17	☐
31	Judges 14	Acts 18	☐

Isaiah 63	Matthew 11	☐
Isaiah 64	Matthew 12	☐
Isaiah 65	Matthew 13	☐
Isaiah 66	Matthew 14	☐
Jeremiah 1	Matthew 15	☐
Jeremiah 2	Matthew 16	☐
Jeremiah 3	Matthew 17	☐
Jeremiah 4	Matthew 18	☐
Jeremiah 5	Matthew 19	☐
Jeremiah 6	Matthew 20	☐
Jeremiah 7	Matthew 21	☐
Jeremiah 8	Matthew 22	☐
Jeremiah 9	Matthew 23	☐
Jeremiah 10	Matthew 24	☐
Jeremiah 11	Matthew 25	☐
Jeremiah 12	Matthew 26	☐
Jeremiah 13	Matthew 27	☐
Jeremiah 14	Matthew 28	☐
Jeremiah 15	Mark 1	☐
Jeremiah 16	Mark 2	☐
Jeremiah 17	Mark 3	☐
Jeremiah 18	Mark 4	☐
Jeremiah 19	Mark 5	☐
Jeremiah 20	Mark 6	☐
Jeremiah 21	Mark 7	☐
Jeremiah 22	Mark 8	☐
Jeremiah 23	Mark 9	☐
Jeremiah 24	Mark 10	☐
Jeremiah 25	Mark 11	☐
Jeremiah 26	Mark 12	☐
Jeremiah 27	Mark 13	☐

1	Judges 15	Acts 19	☐
2	Judges 16	Acts 20	☐
3	Judges 17	Acts 21	☐
4	Judges 18	Acts 22	☐
5	Judges 19	Acts 23	☐
6	Judges 20	Acts 24	☐
7	Judges 21	Acts 25	☐
8	Ruth 1	Acts 26	☐
9	Ruth 2	Acts 27	☐
10	Ruth 3-4	Acts 28	☐
11	1 Samuel 1	Romans 1	☐
12	1 Samuel 2	Romans 2	☐
13	1 Samuel 3	Romans 3	☐
14	1 Samuel 4	Romans 4	☐
15	1 Samuel 5-6	Romans 5	☐
16	1 Samuel 7-8	Romans 6	☐
17	1 Samuel 9	Romans 7	☐
18	1 Samuel 10	Romans 8	☐
19	1 Samuel 11	Romans 9	☐
20	1 Samuel 12	Romans 10	☐
21	1 Samuel 13	Romans 11	☐
22	1 Samuel 14	Romans 12	☐
23	1 Samuel 15	Romans 13	☐
24	1 Samuel 16	Romans 14	☐
25	1 Samuel 17	Romans 15	☐
26	1 Samuel 18	Romans 16	☐
27	1 Samuel 19	1 Corinthians 1	☐
28	1 Samuel 20	1 Corinthians 2	☐
29	1 Samuel 21-22	1 Corinthians 3	☐
30	1 Samuel 23	1 Corinthians 4	☐
31	1 Samuel 24	1 Corinthians 5	☐

Jeremiah 28	Mark 14	☐
Jeremiah 29	Mark 15	☐
Jeremiah 30-31	Mark 16	☐
Jeremiah 32	Psalm 1-2	☐
Jeremiah 33	Psalm 3-4	☐
Jeremiah 34	Psalm 5-6	☐
Jeremiah 35	Psalm 7-8	☐
Jeremiah 36	Psalm 9	☐
Jeremiah 37	Psalm 10	☐
Jeremiah 38	Psalm 11-12	☐
Jeremiah 39	Psalm 13-14	☐
Jeremiah 40	Psalm 15-16	☐
Jeremiah 41	Psalm 17	☐
Jeremiah 42	Psalm 18	☐
Jeremiah 43	Psalm 19	☐
Jeremiah 44-45	Psalm 20-21	☐
Jeremiah 46	Psalm 22	☐
Jeremiah 47	Psalm 23-24	☐
Jeremiah 48	Psalm 25	☐
Jeremiah 49	Psalm 26-27	☐
Jeremiah 50	Psalm 28-29	☐
Jeremiah 51	Psalm 30	☐
Jeremiah 52	Psalm 31	☐
Lamentations 1	Psalm 32	☐
Lamentations 2	Psalm 33	☐
Lamentations 3	Psalm 34	☐
Lamentations 4	Psalm 35	☐
Lamentations 5	Psalm 36	☐
Ezekiel 1	Psalm 37	☐
Ezekiel 2	Psalm 38	☐
Ezekiel 3	Psalm 39	☐

1	1 Samuel 25	1 Corinthians 6	☐
2	1 Samuel 26	1 Corinthians 7	☐
3	1 Samuel 27	1 Corinthians 8	☐
4	1 Samuel 28	1 Corinthians 9	☐
5	1 Samuel 29-30	1 Corinthians 10	☐
6	1 Samuel 31	1 Corinthians 11	☐
7	2 Samuel 1	1 Corinthians 12	☐
8	2 Samuel 2	1 Corinthians 13	☐
9	2 Samuel 3	1 Corinthians 14	☐
10	2 Samuel 4-5	1 Corinthians 15	☐
11	2 Samuel 6	1 Corinthians 16	☐
12	2 Samuel 7	2 Corinthians 1	☐
13	2 Samuel 8-9	2 Corinthians 2	☐
14	2 Samuel 10	2 Corinthians 3	☐
15	2 Samuel 11	2 Corinthians 4	☐
16	2 Samuel 12	2 Corinthians 5	☐
17	2 Samuel 13	2 Corinthians 6	☐
18	2 Samuel 14	2 Corinthians 7	☐
19	2 Samuel 15	2 Corinthians 8	☐
20	2 Samuel 16	2 Corinthians 9	☐
21	2 Samuel 17	2 Corinthians 10	☐
22	2 Samuel 18	2 Corinthians 11	☐
23	2 Samuel 19	2 Corinthians 12	☐
24	2 Samuel 20	2 Corinthians 13	☐
25	2 Samuel 21	Galatians 1	☐
26	2 Samuel 22	Galatians 2	☐
27	2 Samuel 23	Galatians 3	☐
28	2 Samuel 24	Galatians 4	☐
29	1 Kings 1	Galatians 5	☐
30	1 Kings 2	Galatians 6	☐

Ezekiel 4	Psalms 40-41	☐
Ezekiel 5	Psalm 42-43	☐
Ezekiel 6	Psalm 44	☐
Ezekiel 7	Psalm 45	☐
Ezekiel 8	Psalms 46-47	☐
Ezekiel 9	Psalm 48	☐
Ezekiel 10	Psalm 49	☐
Ezekiel 11	Psalm 50	☐
Ezekiel 12	Psalm 51	☐
Ezekiel 13	Psalms 52-54	☐
Ezekiel 14	Psalm 55	☐
Ezekiel 15	Psalms 56-57	☐
Ezekiel 16	Psalm 58-59	☐
Ezekiel 17	Psalm 60-61	☐
Ezekiel 18	Psalm 62-63	☐
Ezekiel 19	Psalm 64-65	☐
Ezekiel 20	Psalm 66-67	☐
Ezekiel 21	Psalm 68	☐
Ezekiel 22	Psalm 69	☐
Ezekiel 23	Psalm 70-71	☐
Ezekiel 24	Psalm 72	☐
Ezekiel 25	Psalm 73	☐
Ezekiel 26	Psalm 74	☐
Ezekiel 27	Psalm 75-76	☐
Ezekiel 28	Psalm 77	☐
Ezekiel 29	Psalm 78:1-39	☐
Ezekiel 30	Psalm 78:40-72	☐
Ezekiel 31	Psalm 79	☐
Ezekiel 32	Psalm 80	☐
Ezekiel 33	Psalm 81-82	☐

1	1 Kings 3	Ephesians 1	☐
2	1 Kings 4-5	Ephesians 2	☐
3	1 Kings 6	Ephesians 3	☐
4	1 Kings 7	Ephesians 4	☐
5	1 Kings 8	Ephesians 5	☐
6	1 Kings 9	Ephesians 6	☐
7	1 Kings 10	Philippians 1	☐
8	1 Kings 11	Philippians 2	☐
9	1 Kings 12	Philippians 3	☐
10	1 Kings 13	Philippians 4	☐
11	1 Kings 14	Colossians 1	☐
12	1 Kings 15	Colossians 2	☐
13	1 Kings 16	Colossians 3	☐
14	1 Kings 17	Colossians 4	☐
15	1 Kings 18	1 Thessalonians 1	☐
16	1 Kings 19	1 Thessalonians 2	☐
17	1 Kings 20	1 Thessalonians 3	☐
18	1 Kings 21	1 Thessalonians 4	☐
19	1 Kings 22	1 Thessalonians 5	☐
20	2 Kings 1	2 Thessalonians 1	☐
21	2 Kings 2	2 Thessalonians 2	☐
22	2 Kings 3	2 Thessalonians 3	☐
23	2 Kings 4	1 Timothy 1	☐
24	2 Kings 5	1 Timothy 2	☐
25	2 Kings 6	1 Timothy 3	☐
26	2 Kings 7	1 Timothy 4	☐
27	2 Kings 8	1 Timothy 5	☐
28	2 Kings 9	1 Timothy 6	☐
29	2 Kings 10-11	2 Timothy 1	☐
30	2 Kings 12	2 Timothy 2	☐
31	2 Kings 13	2 Timothy 3	☐

Ezekiel 34	Psalms 83-84	☐
Ezekiel 35	Psalm 85	☐
Ezekiel 36	Psalm 86	☐
Ezekiel 37	Psalms 87-88	☐
Ezekiel 38	Psalm 89	☐
Ezekiel 39	Psalm 90	☐
Ezekiel 40	Psalm 91	☐
Ezekiel 41	Psalms 92-93	☐
Ezekiel 42	Psalm 94	☐
Ezekiel 43	Psalms 95-96	☐
Ezekiel 44	Psalms 97-98	☐
Ezekiel 45	Psalms 99-101	☐
Ezekiel 46	Psalm 102	☐
Ezekiel 47	Psalm 103	☐
Ezekiel 48	Psalm 104	☐
Daniel 1	Psalm 105	☐
Daniel 2	Psalm 106	☐
Daniel 3	Psalm 107	☐
Daniel 4	Psalms 108-109	☐
Daniel 5	Psalms 110-111	☐
Daniel 6	Psalms 112-113	☐
Daniel 7	Psalms 114-115	☐
Daniel 8	Psalm 116	☐
Daniel 9	Psalms 117-118	☐
Daniel 10	Psalm 119:1-24	☐
Daniel 11	Psalm 119:25-48	☐
Daniel 12	Psalm 119:49-72	☐
Hosea 1	Psalm 119:73-96	☐
Hosea 2	Psalm 119:97-120	☐
Hosea 3-4	Psalm 119:121-144	☐
Hosea 5-6	Psalm 119:145-176	☐

1	2 Kings 14	2 Timothy 4	☐
2	2 Kings 15	Titus 1	☐
3	2 Kings 16	Titus 2	☐
4	2 Kings 17	Titus 3	☐
5	2 Kings 18	Philemon	☐
6	2 Kings 19	Hebrews 1	☐
7	2 Kings 20	Hebrews 2	☐
8	2 Kings 21	Hebrews 3	☐
9	2 Kings 22	Hebrews 4	☐
10	2 Kings 23	Hebrews 5	☐
11	2 Kings 24	Hebrews 6	☐
12	2 Kings 25	Hebrews 7	☐
13	1 Chronicles 1-2	Hebrews 8	☐
14	1 Chronicles 3-4	Hebrews 9	☐
15	1 Chronicles 5-6	Hebrews 10	☐
16	1 Chronicles 7-8	Hebrews 11	☐
17	1 Chronicles 9-10	Hebrews 12	☐
18	1 Chronicles 11-12	Hebrews 13	☐
19	1 Chronicles 13-14	James 1	☐
20	1 Chronicles 15	James 2	☐
21	1 Chronicles 16	James 3	☐
22	1 Chronicles 17	James 4	☐
23	1 Chronicles 18	James 5	☐
24	1 Chronicles 19-20	1 Peter 1	☐
25	1 Chronicles 21	1 Peter 2	☐
26	1 Chronicles 22	1 Peter 3	☐
27	1 Chronicles 23	1 Peter 4	☐
28	1 Chronicles 24-25	1 Peter 5	☐
29	1 Chronicles 26-27	2 Peter 1	☐
30	1 Chronicles 28	2 Peter 2	☐

Hosea 7	Psalms 120-122	☐
Hosea 8	Psalms 123-125	☐
Hosea 9	Psalms 126-128	☐
Hosea 10	Psalms 129-131	☐
Hosea 11	Psalms 132-134	☐
Hosea 12	Psalms 135-136	☐
Hosea 13	Psalms 137-138	☐
Hosea 14	Psalm 139	☐
Joel 1	Psalms 140-141	☐
Joel 2	Psalm 142	☐
Joel 3	Psalm 143	☐
Amos 1	Psalm 144	☐
Amos 2	Psalm 145	☐
Amos 3	Psalms 146-147	☐
Amos 4	Psalms 148-150	☐
Amos 5	Luke 1:1-38	☐
Amos 6	Luke 1:39-80	☐
Amos 7	Luke 2	☐
Amos 8	Luke 3	☐
Amos 9	Luke 4	☐
Obadiah	Luke 5	☐
Jonah 1	Luke 6	☐
Jonah 2	Luke 7	☐
Jonah 3	Luke 8	☐
Jonah 4	Luke 9	☐
Micah 1	Luke 10	☐
Micah 2	Luke 11	☐
Micah 3	Luke 12	☐
Micah 4	Luke 13	☐
Micah 5	Luke 14	☐

1	1 Chronicles 29	2 Peter 3	☐
2	2 Chronicles 1	1 John 1	☐
3	2 Chronicles 2	1 John 2	☐
4	2 Chronicles 3-4	1 John 3	☐
5	2 Chronicles 5-6:11	1 John 4	☐
6	2 Chronicles 6:12-42	1 John 5	☐
7	2 Chronicles 7	2 John	☐
8	2 Chronicles 8	3 John	☐
9	2 Chronicles 9	Jude	☐
10	2 Chronicles 10	Revelation 1	☐
11	2 Chronicles 11-12	Revelation 2	☐
12	2 Chronicles 13	Revelation 3	☐
13	2 Chronicles 14-15	Revelation 4	☐
14	2 Chronicles 16	Revelation 5	☐
15	2 Chronicles 17	Revelation 6	☐
16	2 Chronicles 18	Revelation 7	☐
17	2 Chronicles 19-20	Revelation 8	☐
18	2 Chronicles 21	Revelation 9	☐
19	2 Chronicles 22-23	Revelation 10	☐
20	2 Chronicles 24	Revelation 11	☐
21	2 Chronicles 25	Revelation 12	☐
22	2 Chronicles 26	Revelation 13	☐
23	2 Chronicles 27-28	Revelation 14	☐
24	2 Chronicles 29	Revelation 15	☐
25	2 Chronicles 30	Revelation 16	☐
26	2 Chronicles 31	Revelation 17	☐
27	2 Chronicles 32	Revelation 18	☐
28	2 Chronicles 33	Revelation 19	☐
29	2 Chronicles 34	Revelation 20	☐
30	2 Chronicles 35	Revelation 21	☐
31	2 Chronicles 36	Revelation 22	☐

Micah 6	Luke 15	☐
Micah 7	Luke 16	☐
Nahum 1	Luke 17	☐
Nahum 2	Luke 18	☐
Nahum 3	Luke 19	☐
Habakkuk 1	Luke 20	☐
Habakkuk 2	Luke 21	☐
Habakkuk 3	Luke 22	☐
Zephaniah 1	Luke 23	☐
Zephaniah 2	Luke 24	☐
Zephaniah 3	John 1	☐
Haggai 1	John 2	☐
Haggai 2	John 3	☐
Zechariah 1	John 4	☐
Zechariah 2	John 5	☐
Zechariah 3	John 6	☐
Zechariah 4	John 7	☐
Zechariah 5	John 8	☐
Zechariah 6	John 9	☐
Zechariah 7	John 10	☐
Zechariah 8	John 11	☐
Zechariah 9	John 12	☐
Zechariah 10	John 13	☐
Zechariah 11	John 14	☐
Zechariah 12	John 15	☐
Zechariah 13	John 16	☐
Zechariah 14	John 17	☐
Malachi 1	John 18	☐
Malachi 2	John 19	☐
Malachi 3	John 20	☐
Malachi 4	John 21	☐

WHO WE ARE

Dictum was founded in 2018, and is based in Oxford. It publishes books for the West and the Global South which are biblical, pastoral and incisive. Dictum's lists (see over) include classic reprints. Churches or agencies ordering in bulk, perhaps for a special event or anniversary, are invited to add their logo and a description of their ministry at the front of titles purchased. Review copies are available at no charge. For more, visit *dictumpress.com*

The Evangelical Fellowship in the Anglican Communion (EFAC) was founded with prescience in 1961 by John Stott. EFAC works to enable Anglican leaders around the world to stand firm, to engage thoughtfully with secular trends, and to articulate a persuasive biblical response to them. Its Theology Resource Network (TRN) draws senior theologians from all continents. The Church of England Evangelical Council (CEEC) is its affiliated group in England. To learn more, and to view their publications, visit *efacglobal.com* and *ceec.info*

'Clarity and brevity are two great gifts to the world.'

Dictum's books do not waste words, or waste the reader's time. They bring biblical thinking which is refreshing, clear and well-applied.

Dictum has four lists:

Dictum Essentials: Core books for wide use in churches and mission agencies, with questions for personal reflection or discussion.

Oxbridge: Church history from the ancient university towns of Oxford and Cambridge. Including a Reformation Walking Tour; and a humorous feline view of Oxford.

Unique angles on John Stott's ministry, including the remarkable story of Frances Whitehead, his secretary for 55 years, a story which needs to be preserved; and a fun authorized children's biography.

List Four: A growing and diverse wider list of pithy books, longer and shorter.

dictumpress.com
books worth reading more than once